Writing to
CORRESPOND

Jill Jarnow

The Rosen Publishing Group's
PowerKids Press™
New York

Published in 2006 by The Rosen Publishing Group, Inc.
29 East 21st Street, New York, NY 10010

First Edition

Editor: Frances E. Ruffin
Book Design: Emily Muschinske

Photo Credits: Cover images, p. 5 (top) © Corbis; p. 5 (bottom)
© Rijksmuseum Kroller-Muller, Otterlo, Netherlands/Bridgeman Art
Library; p. 9 © Library of Congress, Prints & Photographs Division;
p. 19 © Joseph Muschinske.

Library of Congress Cataloging-in-Publication Data

Jarnow, Jill.
Writing to correspond / Jill Jarnow.
    p. cm. — (Write now: a kid's guide to nonfiction writing)
Summary: Introduces the techniques of letter writing including the
heading, style, addressing an envelope and more.
Includes bibliographical references and index.
ISBN 1-4042-2831-4 (library binding) — ISBN 1-4042-5318-1 (pbk.)
1. Letter writing—Juvenile literature. 2. English language—Composition
and exercises—Juvenile literature. [1. Letter writing.] I. Title.

PE1483.J37 2005
808.6—dc22
                                        2003018671

Manufactured in the United States of America

Contents

Writing to Correspond

Writing a letter is a good way to ask someone a question, to tell someone good news, or to invite a friend to a party. Corresponding, or writing letters, is a great way to **communicate**. A letter allows you to organize your words so that you can send a message that is strong and clear. Letters and other forms of correspondence give us a written record of how people lived in the past. In this book you will learn how to write business letters and **personal** letters, which include thank-you notes, fan letters, and invitations. You will also learn how to address an **envelope** so that your letter reaches the right person!

This letter (right) was written by President John F. Kennedy (above), who called himself Jack. He wrote to his father when he was 12 years old. Kennedy asked his father to increase his allowance. He wrote, "My recent allowance is 40 [cents]. This I used for [airplanes] and other playthings."

Petit-Wasmes
June 1879

Dear Theo:

A few days ago, we had a very heavy thunderstorm at about eleven o'clock in the evening. Quite near our house there is a spot from which one can see, far below, a large part of the Borinage, with the chimneys, the mounds of coal, the little miners' cottages, the scurrying black figures by day, like ants in a nest. . . .

Your loving brother,

Vincent

Artist Vincent van Gogh once lived in a coal-mining area in Belgium. In a letter to his brother, Vincent described scenes that appear in some of his paintings, such as Miners' Wives Carrying Sacks of Coal (1882), shown above. In this example, the letter has been changed to English.

The Parts of a Personal Letter

Every letter that you write should have a heading at the top of the paper. It should include your address and the date. Each letter should also include a **salutation**, or greeting. A personal greeting usually starts with the word "Dear" and ends with the person's name followed by a comma. Begin each word in the greeting with a capital letter. The body of the letter is where you write what you want to say. The closing, which ends with a comma, is where you say good-bye. Begin the closing with a capital letter.

Check It Out!

E-mail is one way to correspond with people. You do not need to include a heading as in a letter, but all other rules apply.

Writing a Personal Letter

5 Berry Lane
City, State Zip Code

The heading should be in the upper left or right side of the paper.

Date

Dear Katie,

In a personal letter, end the greeting with a comma.

I am so glad that you, Aunt Anna, and Uncle Bill are coming to spend Labor Day weekend with us. I have planned lots of things for us to do while you are here. One thing we are going to do is to watch the boat race on the river. Then we will go to an ice cream festival. This is a really yummy party! I really can't wait!

Body of the letter

Love,

Jeannie

Your cousin Jeannie

If you are typing your letter, skip four lines after the closing and type your name. Then sign your name above your typed name. This is called your signature.

The Business Letter

When you write a business letter, state what you need at the beginning of the letter and stick to one subject. People usually write business letters to give or get **information** or to ask for help. Before you write your business letter, plan what you want to say.

Your business letter should be clear and easy to understand. For example, if you need information to write a report, explain in **detail** what you need to know. If you are writing about a problem, describe it in the first sentence, if possible. Suggest a way to help fix it. Then end your letter by thanking the reader for his or her help.

Civil War photographer Mathew Brady wrote this business letter to President Abraham Lincoln. Brady asked Lincoln to sit for a photograph. Lincoln agreed, and the photo was taken (inset). The Civil War was fought between the Northern and Southern states from 1861 to 1865.

In a business letter today, one would normally include the address of the person to whom the letter is being sent. This is called the inside address.

Brady's Gallery
352 Pennsylvania Avenue
Washington, D.C.
March 2, 1865

The heading

Mr. President,
Dear Sir:

The greeting in a business letter ends with a colon.

I have repeated calls every hour in the day for your photograph. And [I] would regard it as a great honor if you could give me a sitting today so that I may be able to exhibit a large picture on the 4th. If you cannot call today please call at your earliest convenience. . . .

State your business right away.

Yours truly,
M. B. Brady

Writing a Business Letter

Prepare a **draft** of your business letter before you write the letter. Keep handy the address of the person to whom you are writing. You will need it for the heading. Make an **outline** of your business letter by listing the facts, ideas, or questions that you want to include. Number the items on your list in the order in which they will appear in your letter. Then write a first draft of the business letter. Read the draft to add or to rearrange information. Shorten and smooth your sentences. Correct facts and spelling. Be sure that your **punctuation** is correct. Make a neat, clean final draft.

A Business Letter

Out of this World Catalog
Customer Service Department
100 Industrial Way
City, State Zip

Headings in some business letters appear in the upper right side of the letter.

Sally Salton
100 East 13th Street
City, State Zip Code

The inside address

Date

To Whom It May Concern:

End a business greeting with a colon. Be sure to capitalize the first letters of each word in the greeting.

ordered

I recently ~~mailed you an order for~~ a ring from your catalog. It was item number B-1001. I received ~~instead~~ glow-in-the-dark shoelaces instead of the ring. The item number for the shoelaces is B-1011. Please send me the decoder ring as soon as possible so that I can use it for my project on spies. I will return the shoelaces as soon as possible. Thank you for your help.

decoder ring

Make changes so that your letter is clear and easy to understand.

Yours

Sincerely ~~yours~~,

Sally Salton

Sally Salton

Capitalize all of the words in the closing of a business letter.

Writing a Fan Letter

Is there someone you really **admire**, such as a favorite book author, a sports figure, the president, or even a member of your family? You can write that person a fan letter to explain why you admire him or her. When you correspond with someone you admire, keep your letter short and to the point. Describe in a few sentences what he or she has done that pleases you. Be **sincere**. If you are corresponding with someone famous and you would like the person to answer your letter, ask a question. This makes it easier for the person to write back to you.

A Fan Letter

Peter Granger
Granger, Tocas & Partners
10 Madison Circle
City, State Zip

Date

Dear Uncle Peter,

Thank you for taking me to see the Wilson house getting built last Saturday. Whenever I visit your office you take the time to show me the plans and drawings for the projects that you are working on. Saturday was the first time I saw your design become a real house. Since then, I have made an important decision. Someday, I want to become an architect like you. I love to make buildings with plastic blocks, and I love to draw, so I think that I will be a good architect. I hope my plans will be as wonderful as yours.

Love,

Jason

In a fan letter, use a personal greeting. For a person you do not know, use a title, such as Mr. or Mrs.

Explain why you admire the person. Give examples.

Be sure to sign your first and last name in a letter to someone you do not know personally.

How to Address an Envelope

The address on the front of an envelope tells the mail carrier where to bring your letter. On the first line of the address, write the name of the person who will receive the letter. Write that person's street address on the second line. Include the house or apartment number. On the third line, write the town or city, the state, and the zip code. Write your return address in the upper left corner of the envelope. Put your stamp on the upper right corner of the envelope.

Check It Out!

Zip codes are important! Mail carriers read an address on an envelope from the bottom up.

Addressing an Envelope

Address envelopes in black or dark blue ink.

Write your return address in the upper left corner of the envelope.

Use capital letters and two-letter codes for states. For example, the two-letter code for Rhode Island is RI.

Sara Ann Thomas
148 Garden Street
City, State Zip code

PLACE
STAMP
HERE

Mr. John Alexander
12 Kennedy Court, 3G
City, State Zip Code

PLACE
STAMP
HERE

Phyliss Watson
22 Belle Drive
City, State Zip Code

Ms. Elizabeth Martin
Vice President, Production
Daisy Designs
859 Broadway Drive
City, State Zip Code

Put a stamp in the upper right corner of the envelope.

If you are sending a business letter, add the person's job title.

File This...

If your letter is going to another country, write the country's name and zone, which is like an American zip code, on the bottom line.

15

Writing a Thank-You Note

When someone does something nice for you or gives you a gift, send a thank-you note! Writing a thank-you note lets the person know that the gift or the help was **appreciated**. In a sentence or two, describe how the help made a difference, or tell how the gift will be used. For example, tell your grandmother why you like the sweater that she sent you for your birthday. Even if you do not like the present, write your thanks. Use friendly language to thank a friend or a relative. To thank a business person, set up your letter in the business style used on page 8.

Thanks Dad!

Date

Dear Dad,

Thank you SO much for buying me a jar of Cozy Kitchen peanut butter. It's my favorite food in the whole world. I appreciate that you drove all the way to Easton Farms just to get it, especially since it was your day off!

My peanut butter and jelly sandwich tasted super yummy today. I'm going to eat the peanut butter slowly so that the jar will last a long time. Thanks for thinking of me. You're the best dad in the world.

Hugs and Kisses,

Margery

There is no need for a heading in a thank-you note.

Describe in one or two sentences what a person has done to receive your thanks.

Be sure to tell the person how you will use the gift.

Use a personal voice to thank a friend or a relative.

Letters to the Editor

People write letters to newspaper **editors** to give opinions, to voice **complaints**, and to suggest ways to make changes. Sometimes people write letters to an editor to **praise** a person or an event.

Use a business style to write your letter to the editor of a newspaper. Begin by writing your opinion. Support your opinions with facts. Always use a writing style that is **polite** by choosing words that are respectful. Mail your letter to the editor, whose name you will find on the **masthead** of the editorial page of the newspaper.

A Letter to the Editor

The Fifth Street School
190 Fifth Street
Sunville, State   Zip Code

Date

Jack Hawthorne, Editor
The Sunville Times
1225 Boulder Road
Sunville, State Zip Code

Dear Mr. Hawthorne:

I am the president of Fifth Street School's student board. We have noticed that there are many homeless cats and dogs in town. We feel that our town should have its own shelter where animals could live until new homes could be found for them.

We would like to ask other schools in Sunville to help us raise money to build a shelter. We could hold bake sales, put on plays, or wash cars. We hope that Mayor Bean or another member of the town council will help us with this project.

Sincerely,

Jean Austin

Jean Austin

A business letter in which everything lines up along the left side of the paper is called block style.

Use business-style punctuation in the greeting and closing.

State the reason you are writing.

Tell the reader how he or she can help.

By Special Invitation

Everyone likes to receive an invitation to a party or to a special event. You can buy invitations on which are printed the 5Ws: What kind of party or event is it? Who is the party for? Why is the event being held? Where and when will the event take place? All you have to do is fill in the information. You can also make your own invitations. Invitations often ask people to RSVP. In French, this stands for *réspondez s'il vous plaît*. In English, this means "please tell me whether you can come," or "please reply." When you include "RSVP" at the bottom of an invitation, be sure to include your phone number or e-mail address.

A Cruise
for a
Graduate!

You are invited to a graduation party for

Darcy Schoefield

When: 2:00 P.M. until 7:00 P.M. on May 14

Where: The Three Rivers Boat Club
Ocean City, State   Zip Code

Sailing time is 2:15 P.M. sharp!

To hold your spot, please RSVP.
555-7777

Be sure to include the date, location, and time on your invitation.

Include a phone number or an e-mail address if you want a reply.

Making a Poster or a Flyer

Are you holding a yard sale? Are you running for class president? Make your **announcement** in a striking way with a poster or a flyer. Posters are usually large, stiff pieces of poster board. Flyers are letter-size announcements. At the top of the poster, write your information in large letters to catch people's attention. Use the 5Ws to describe the reason for the event. Give the date, place, and time of the event, as well as your phone number if you need people to contact you. Let people know if they must pay to attend an event, and how much it will cost. Keep information in the notice short and to the point.

Glossary

admire (ad-MYR) To respect or look up to.

announcement (uh-NOWN-sment) A statement.

appreciated (uh-PREE-shee-ayt-ed) To have been thankful for something or someone.

communicate (kuh-MYOO-nih-kayt) To share facts or feelings.

complaints (kum-PLAYNTS) Statements that something is wrong.

detail (DEE-tayl) Extra fact.

draft (DRAFT) A nonfinal copy, plan, or drawing.

editors (EH-dih-terz) The people who correct errors, check facts, and decide what will be printed in a newspaper, book, or magazine.

envelope (EN-veh-lohp) A cover used for mailing a letter.

information (in-fer-MAY-shun) Knowledge or facts.

masthead (MAST-hed) A list in a newspaper or magazine that tells who the owner and editors are.

outline (OWT-lyn) A written description that includes the main points of a paper.

personal (PERS-nul) Describing the private matters of a person.

polite (puh-LYT) To behave well in front of others.

praise (PRAYZ) To say nice things about someone.

punctuation (punk-choo-WAY-shun) The use of periods, commas, and other marks to help make the meaning of a sentence clear.

salutation (sal-yoo-TAY-shun) Greeting.

sincere (sin-SEER) Honest about one's feelings.

Index

Web Sites

Due to the changing nature of Internet links, PowerKids Press has developed an online list of Web sites related to the subject of this book. This site is updated regularly. Please use this link to access the list:
www.powerkidslinks.com/wnkw/writcorr/